Literature Guide for Tuck Everlasting

By Natalie Babbitt

A Study Guide Prepared by
Melissa Eydenberg and Rebecca Stark

The purchase of this book entitles the individual teacher to reproduce copies of the student pages for use in his or her classroom exclusively. The reproduction of any part of the work for an entire school or school system or for commercial use is prohibited.

ISBN 978-1-56644-575-7

© 2016 Barbara M. Peller

Educational Books 'n' Bingo

Previously published by Educational Impressions, Inc.

Printed in the U.S.A.

Tuck Everlasting
Written by Natalie Babbitt

STORY SUMMARY

Ten-year-old Winnie Foster is looking for adventure. She wants to "make some kind of difference in the world." Winnie feels trapped—cooped up—as if her yard were a cage and her mother and grandmother her keepers.

Winnie finds the adventure she seeks when she encounters the Tuck family. The Tucks unknowingly drank from a magical spring that blessed—or cursed—them with eternal life. They are truly trapped—frozen in their current stages of life, unable to grow or change!

Winnie's adventure peaks when Mae Tuck kills a man because he intends to force Winnie to drink the magical water. Mae is sentenced to hang, but Winnie helps her escape from jail. Ironically, the Tucks also have helped free Winnie from her feelings of being trapped.

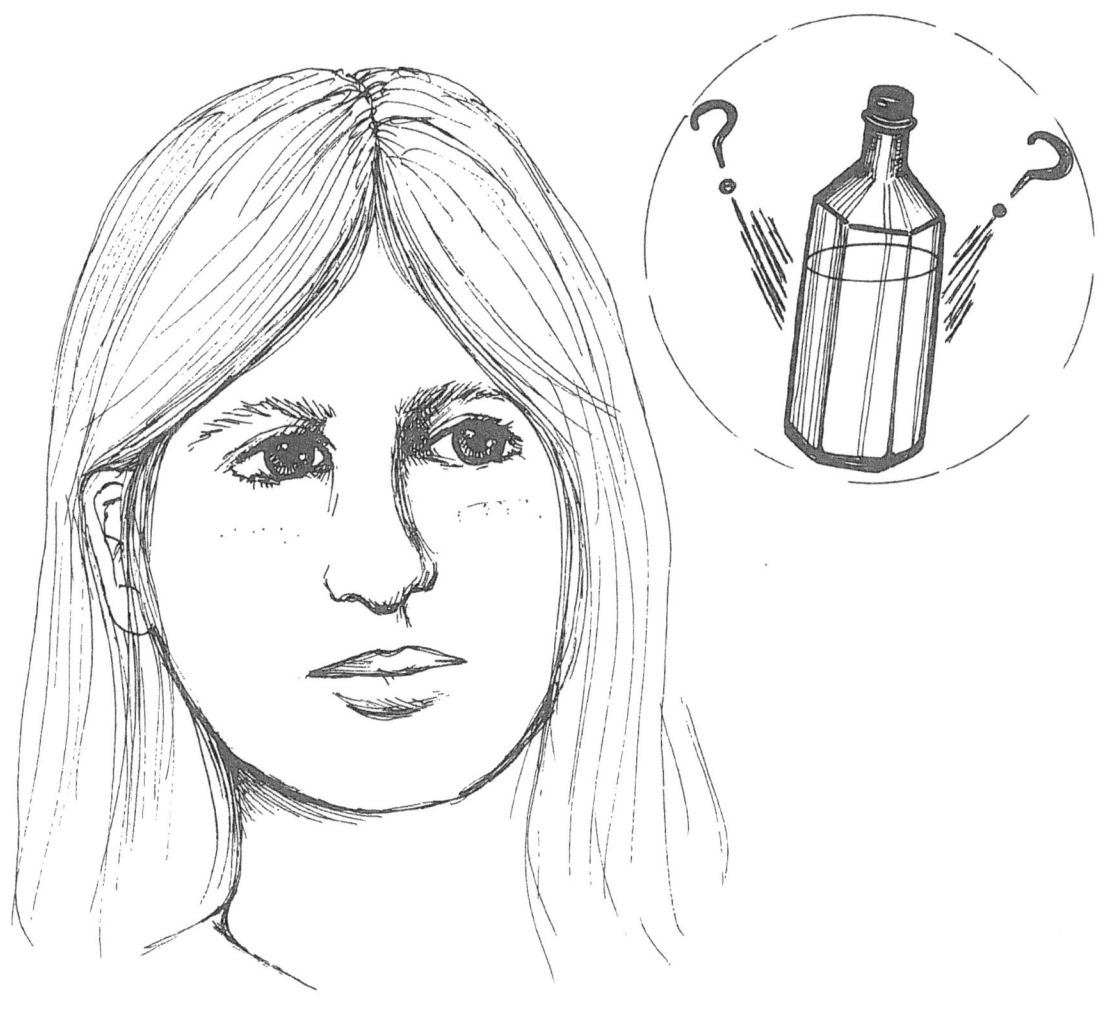

© 1996 Educational Impressions, Inc.

Meet the Author
Natalie Babbitt

Born Natalie Zane Moore on July 28, 1932, in Dayton, Ohio, Natalie formed an early interest in books. Although she is now appreciated as an accomplished author, she began her career as an artist and illustrator.

Natalie studied art at Smith College, where she met Samuel Babbitt, an aspiring writer. The two were married in 1954. Samuel shared her interests, and while she raised their children, he worked as a writer. In fact, his efforts as an author helped foster Natalie's career as an illustrator. In 1966 she illustrated *The Forty-Ninth Magician,* which was written by Samuel. The success of this book encouraged her to produce children's books on her own.

Many of Babbitt's stories playfully use fantasy to illustrate a moral lesson. Her stories appear on the surface to be aimed at children, but the serious underlying subject matter also offers more mature readers interesting material.

Natalie Babbitt has written several award-winning novels for young people. Among her most popular are *Kneeknock Rise,* published in 1971; *Tuck Everlasting,* published in 1975; and *The Eyes of the Amaryllis,* published in 1977. *Kneeknock Rise* was selected as a Newbery Honor Book.

Pre-Reading Activity
The 1880s

Tuck Everlasting flashes back to the 1880s. With your cooperative-learning group, brainstorm a list of things you use every day that did not exist in the 1880s.

Using the list compiled by your group, decide which ten things you would miss most if you were transported back in time to 1880. Rate them from 1 to 10, with 1 being the item you would miss the most.

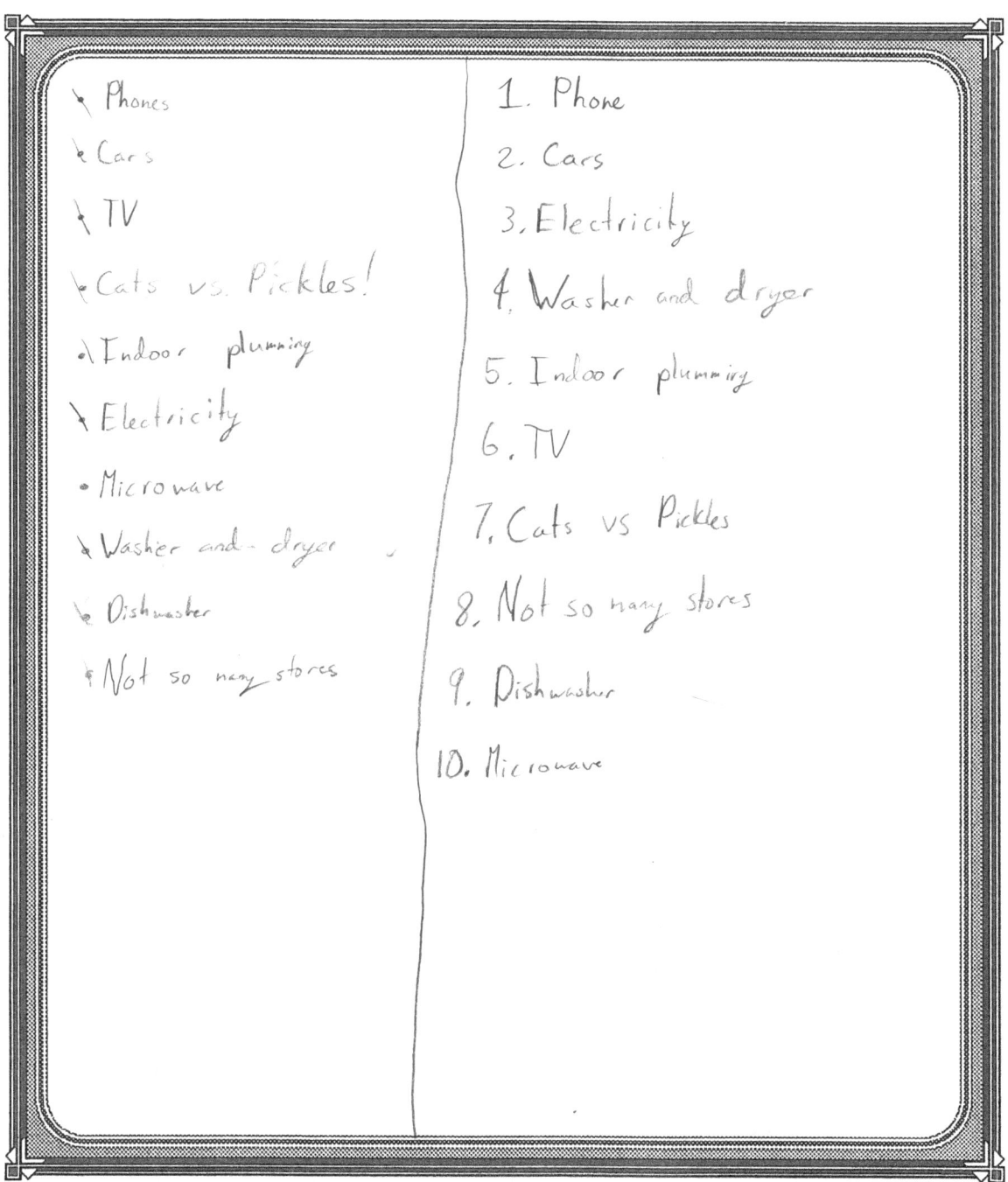

© 1996 Educational Impressions, Inc.

Vocabulary
Prologue and Chapters One and Two

Use the words in the box to complete the sentences. You may need to use your dictionary.

ambled	axis	balmy	bovine	forlorn
fringe	grubs	immense	meager	melancholy
quivers	rueful	tangent	trod	veered

1. We enjoyed the _____ breeze on the mild, pleasant day.
2. Just before my baby brother cries, his lower lip _____.
3. Brian's wrinkled shirt looks like a herd of wild horses _____ upon it.
4. "Just stick to the subject," said Miss Grey. "Don't go off on a _____."
5. The bedspread was blue and had _____ that reached the floor.
6. Feline refers to cats; _____ refers to cows.
7. Michael's sled _____ off the path and hit a tree.
8. We weren't in a hurry, so we _____ along the boulevard.
9. Breakfast was _____ fare of toast and juice.
10. When his family left him alone, the boy felt _____.
11. The wormlike _____ were in the garden.
12. The hole was so _____ that all the children fit in it.
13. A top spins on its _____.
14. The song was so _____ that it made me cry.
15. She had such a _____ look that I could not help but pity her.

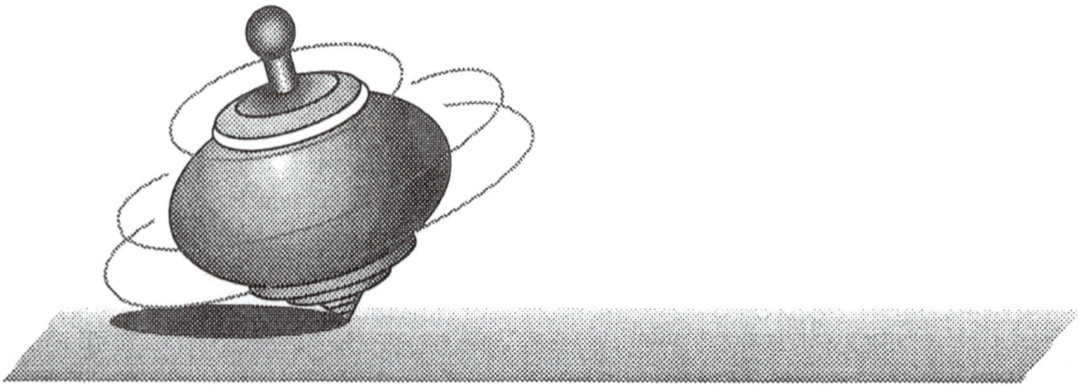

6 *Tuck Everlasting* © 1996 Educational Impressions, Inc.

Comprehension and Discussion Questions
Prologue and Chapters One and Two

Answer the following questions in complete sentence form. Give examples from the story to support your response.

PROLOGUE

1. Find out what is meant by "the dog days." Use what you learn to explain the author's simile in which she compared the first week of August to a seat on a ferris wheel.

2. What three events took place as the story began? What connected these events?

3. What was at the center, or hub, of the narrator's wheel? What, do you think, does the wheel itself represent?

CHAPTER ONE

1. What was strange about the wood? What effect did it have on passersby? What effect did it have on the cows?

© 1996 Educational Impressions, Inc.   Tuck Everlasting 7

2. According to the narrator, why wasn't Winnie curious about the wood? Do you agree with this generalization?

3. There are many examples of personification in this chapter. Define *personification*. Cite examples in which the road, the grass, the house, and the wood are personified.

CHAPTER TWO

1. Why had Tuck been smiling?

2. What did Mae take with her? Why?

3. What surprise did we learn at the end of this chapter?

8 *Tuck Everlasting* © 1996 Educational Impressions, Inc.

Vocabulary
Chapters Three, Four, and Five

Use your dictionary to define the following words. Then use the words (or forms of the words) and their definitions to create a crossword puzzle.

abreast	bristly	consolingly	dangled
exasperated	galling	grimace	hysterical
jaunty	peering	persisted	plaintively
primly	pruned	remnants	retorted
self-deprication	solemnly	squinted	venture

Create a Crossword Puzzle

Use the vocabulary words from the first part of this activity to create a crossword puzzle. Try to use all of them! Write the clues on another piece of paper. Number the boxes horizontally and vertically. Darken the boxes that you are not using. Exchange with a classmate to solve!

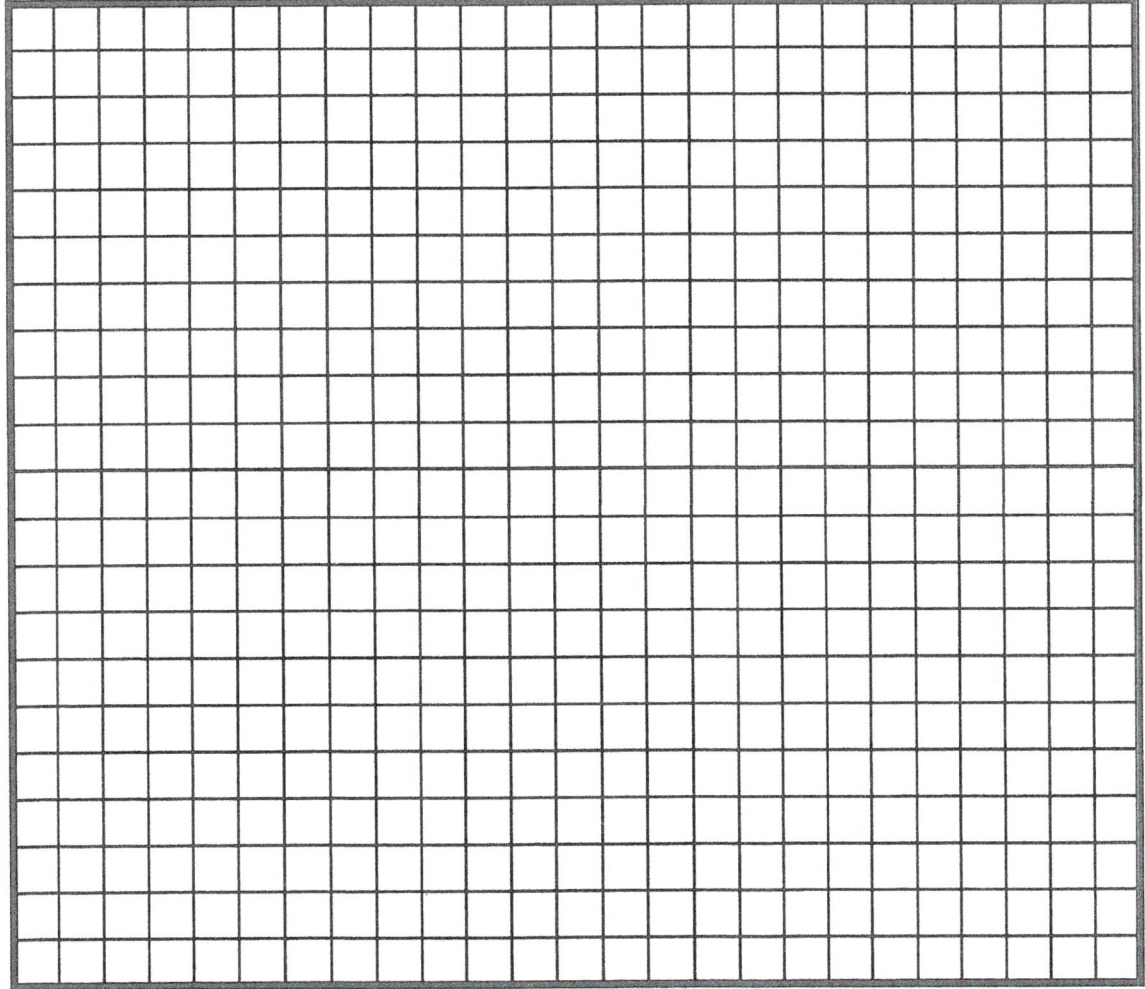

© 1996 Educational Impressions, Inc.

Tuck Everlasting 9

Comprehension and Discussion Questions
Chapters Three, Four, and Five

Answer the following questions in complete sentence form. Give examples from the story to support your response.

CHAPTER THREE

1. To whom did Winnie voice her frustrations. Evaluate her choice.

2. Why did Winnie wish she had a brother or a sister?

3. Predict whether or not Winnie will really run away. Explain your opinion.

CHAPTER FOUR

1. Something happened that makes the reader a little uneasy about the stranger. Explain.

2. Winnie's grandmother believed that the music they heard was elf music. What was it really? When had her grandmother heard the music before?

3. Guess why the stranger had an expression of intense satisfaction.

CHAPTER FIVE

1. What prompted Winnie to venture into the wood for the first time?

2. Why were the pebbles piled upon the spurt of water?

3. Guess why Jesse wouldn't let Winnie have any of the water. What do you think he meant when he said, "I knew this would happen sooner or later"?

Vocabulary
Chapters Six, Seven, and Eight

Read each clue and find the answers in the box. Then use the letters above the numbered spaces to decipher the secret message.

> burly   conclusion   crept
> graze   harness   knobby
> parson   populated   troupe   whoop

1. a company or group   __ __ __ __ __ __
                        21   3
2. strong and muscular __ __ __ __ __
                           5 19
3. gear for a draft animal __ __ __ __ __ __ __
                             2   20   16
4. having a rounded bulge __ __ __ __ __ __
                           7   13
5. inhabited __ __ __ __ __ __ __ __ __
                              4   11
6. to feed on growing grass __ __ __ __ __
                             15 12
7. a judgment or decision __ __ __ __ __ __ __ __ __ __
                           6   14
8. a clergyman __ __ __ __ __ __
                10   8
9. a cry of excitement __ __ __ __ __
                        9
10. moved cautiously __ __ __ __ __
                      18 17   1

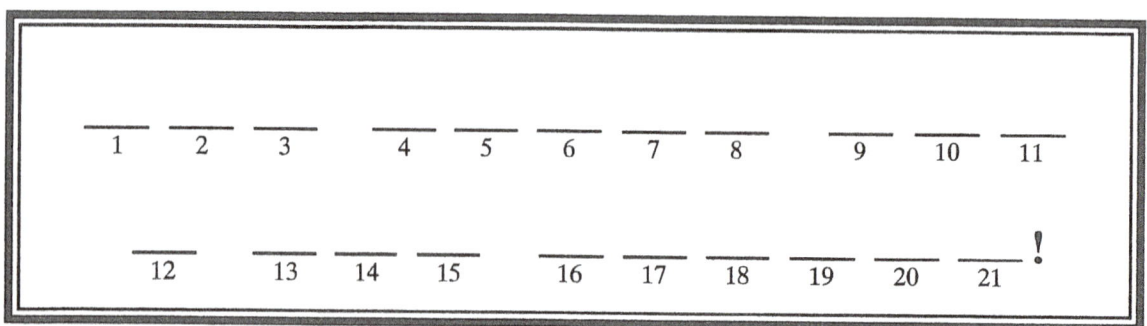

Comprehension and Discussion Questions
Chapters Six, Seven, and Eight

Answer the following questions in complete sentence form. Give examples from the story to support your response.

CHAPTER SIX

1. Contrast Winnie's kidnapping with the way Winnie had envisioned a kidnapping.

2. Why did Winnie begin to cry? How did Mae console her?

3. Why, do you think, did the Tucks avoid having a plan of action in case they were discovered?

CHAPTER SEVEN

1. Why did Miles's wife take the children and leave him?

2. What led the Tucks to conclude that the spring water was the source of their immortality?

3. How did Tuck prove beyond doubt his immortality? Judge this action.

_____
_____
_____
_____

CHAPTER EIGHT

1. Mae said to Winnie, "We'll bring you back tomorrow. All right?" Winnie answered, "All right." In your opinion, what would have happened if Winnie had answered, "No"?

_____
_____
_____
_____

2. Describe the way the Tucks made Winnie feel.

_____
_____
_____
_____

3. In addition to Winnie, who heard the whole story about the spring? Predict what he will do.

_____
_____
_____
_____

Vocabulary
Chapters Nine, Ten, and Eleven

Match the vocabulary words on the left to the definitions on the right. Place the correct letter on each line.

____ 1. vanity   A. inflated pride
____ 2. revive   B. like a cavern in depth or vastness
____ 3. rutted   C. a fluttering sound
____ 4. embankment   D. to return to life; to resuscitate
____ 5. assaults   E. of the most expensive and choice variety
____ 6. scour   F. moved hurriedly
____ 7. indomitable   G. grooved as a result of passage of time
____ 8. eddy   H. an optical illusion
____ 9. strewn   I. a rescuer from dire circumstances
____ 10. helter-skelter J. a state of disorder
____ 11. cavernous   K. a mound of earth to support a roadway
____ 12. camphor   L. extreme joy
____ 13. mirage   M. violent attacks
____ 14. trill   N. a current that moves against main current
____ 15. disarray   O. haphazardly; in disorderly haste
____ 16. hustled   P. to scrub vigorously
____ 17. luxurious   Q. resolute; firm
____ 18. elation   R. incapable of being overcome; unconquerable
____ 19. savior   S. a crystalline compound used as insect repellent
____ 20. decisive   T. scattered

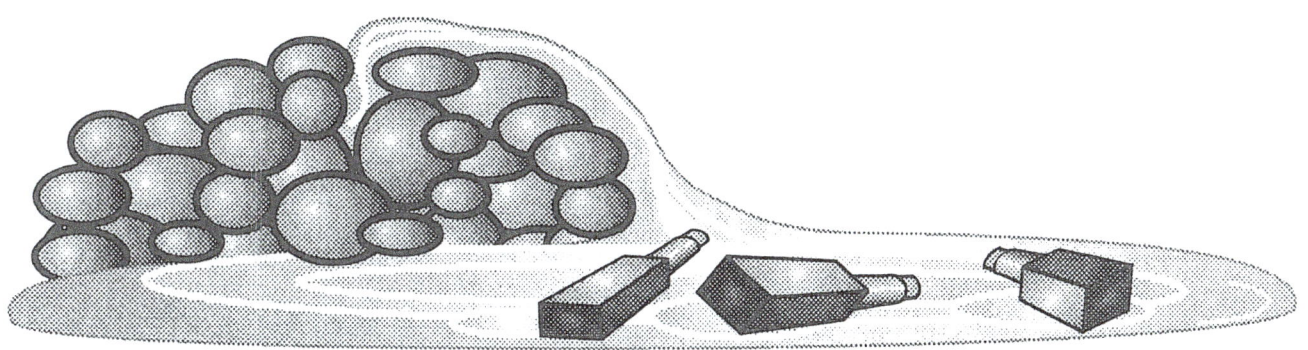

© 1996 Educational Impressions, Inc.   Tuck Everlasting 15

Comprehension and Discussion Questions
Chapters Nine, Ten, and Eleven

Answer the following questions in complete sentence form. Give examples from the story to support your response.

CHAPTER NINE

1. The long journey exhausted Winnie. How did Mae and Miles help?

2. Upon seeing Winnie, Tuck smiled. Why was this unusual?

3. How did Tuck make Winnie feel?

CHAPTER TEN

1. What surprised Winnie most about the Tucks' house?

2. How long had the Tucks lived in this house? Why would they probably move soon?

3. Mae said that Jesse and Miles were somewhat different and, therefore, didn't always get along. Cite examples of those differences.

CHAPTER ELEVEN

1. What seemed strange to Winnie about supper with the Tucks?

2. What caused Winnie's elation to collapse?

3. Why did the thought of the man in the yellow suit cause Winnie to feel a surge of relief?

Vocabulary
Chapters Twelve, Thirteen, and Fourteen

Use your dictionary to define the followng words as they were used in these chapters.

1. anguish
2. anxiously
3. brambles
4. drifted
5. earnestly
6. hoarser
7. lingered
8. outrage
9. rigid
10. ragged
11. silhouettes
12. silty
13. skittering
14. stern
15. strode

Captive!

Imagine that you are Winnie. You know that your family must be very worried about you. Write a letter home to reassure them that you are all right. Include at least five vocabulary words from the first part of this activity.

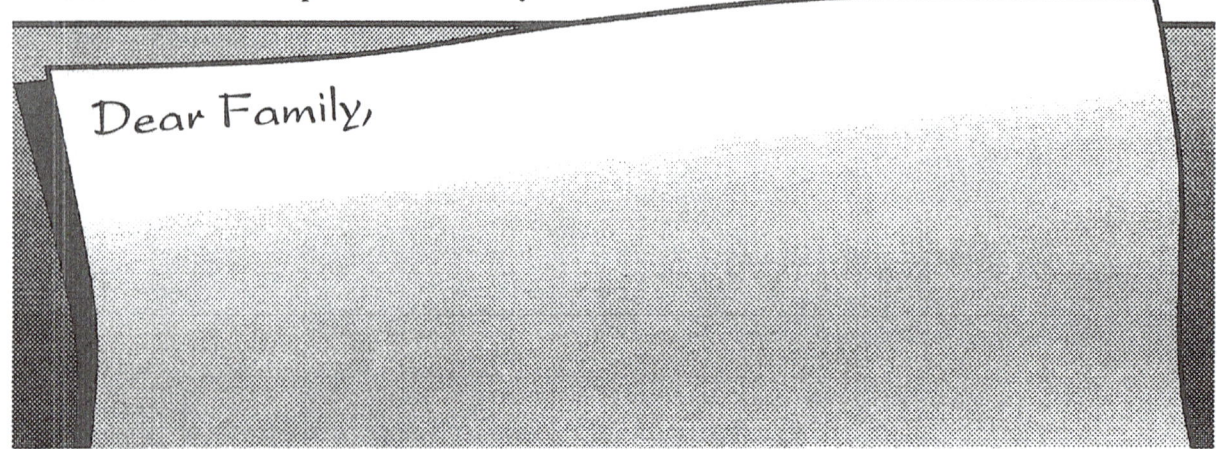

Dear Family,

18 *Tuck Everlasting* © 1996 Educational Impressions, Inc.

Comprehension and Discussion Questions
Chapters Twelve, Thirteen, and Fourteen

Answer the following questions in complete sentence form. Give examples from the story to support your response.

CHAPTER TWELVE

1. Tuck used a metaphor by comparing his family to a rowboat. Explain.

2. Judge Tuck's statement about life: You can't pick out the pieces you like and leave out the rest.

3. What do you think would happen if word got out about the powers of the spring?

CHAPTER THIRTEEN

1. Why were the lights on in the Fosters' home although it was very late?

CHAPTER FOURTEEN

1. The author used foreshadowing at the beginning of this chapter. Explain.

© 1996 Educational Impressions, Inc.

2. What made Winnie feel homesick?

3. What made Winnie feel guilty?

4. Judge Jesse's suggestion. Do you think he had Winnie's best interests in mind?

Vocabulary
Chapters Fifteen, Sixteen, and Seventeen

Alphabetize the following words. Then use your dictionary to define them as they were used in these chapters.

suspended	barbarian	crinkling	illiterates
character	constable	ordeal	wheezed	roust
courteous	accomodations	flanks	cantering	peculiar
threadbare	peril	searing	grudgingly	

Have I Got News For You!

Suppose Miles had told his wife and children about the spring when he first learned of its powers and that he had offered them a drink from it. Keep in mind the ages of his wife and children when Miles learned the truth. As his wife or child, write a letter to Miles explaining why you will or will not accept his offer. Use vocabulary words from the first part of this activity.

© 1996 Educational Impressions, Inc.

Comprehension and Discussion Questions
Chapters Fifteen, Sixteen, and Seventeen

Answer the following questions in complete sentence form. Give examples from the story to support your response.

CHAPTER FIFTEEN

1. What deal did the man in the yellow suit propose to the Fosters?

2. Do you think the agreement would hold up in a court of law? Explain.

3. Why, do you think, did the man want the wood? Surmise what would happen if he got it.

CHAPTER SIXTEEN

1. What excuse did the man in the yellow suit give for not reporting the kidnapping sooner?

2. What caused the constable's eyes to go round?

Tuck Everlasting © 1996 Educational Impressions, Inc.

3. Did you believe the man in the yellow suit when he said, " 'So I'll go on ahead and wait outside the house till you get there' "?

CHAPTER SEVENTEEN

1. Judge Miles's decision not to try to find his family when he learned about the spring.

2. Why did Winnie insist that Miles let the fish go free?

3. Think about Miles's statement: " 'It's no good hiding yourself away, like Pa and lots of other people. And it's no good just thinking of your own pleasure, either. People got to do something useful if they're going to take up space in the world.' " Whom would you be like in a similar situation: Miles, Pa, Jesse, or Mae? Explain.

Vocabulary
Chapters Eighteen, Nineteen, and Twenty

Choose the word or phrase in each set that is **most like** the first word in meaning.

1. **fluttering:**   flying   quivering   soaring
2. **alien:**   friendly   alike   strange
3. **fleeting:**   passing   floating   flashing
4. **legends:**   prayers   stories   laws
5. **route:**   course   defeat   destination
6. **ignorant:**   rude   uneducated   intelligent
7. **petulance:**   irritability   tenderness   loyalty
8. **shrilled:**   whispered   murmured   shouted
9. **sprawled:**   spotted   spread   sputtered
10. **resentfully:**   happily   bitterly   similarly
11. **clutching:**   throwing   dropping   holding
12. **coarse:**   rough   smooth   damp

A Word Game

Get into teams of two or three students. Choose two vocabulary words from the first part of this activity. For each word, see how many little words you can form by using only the letters in that word.

EXAMPLE:

PHILOSOPHY

pop	lip	hop	oil	pool	silo
lisp	sop	hip	slip	spool	soil
his	ploy	pop	loop	yip	spoil

and so on.

Comprehension and Discussion Questions
Chapters Eighteen, Nineteen, and Twenty

Answer the following questions in complete sentence form. Give examples from the story to support your response.

CHAPTER EIGHTEEN

1. Why, do you think, was Winnie's stomach fluttering?

2. Who was "the dearest of them all" to Winnie? Why, do you suppose, did she feel this way?

3. Why would a knock at the door cause Mae to drop her fork?

CHAPTER NINETEEN

1. How did the man in the yellow suit first learn about the Tucks?

2. How might the story have differed if Mae hadn't brought the music box with her when she went to meet her sons?

© 1996 Educational Impressions, Inc.

3. Describe the plan of the man in the yellow suit. How did the Tucks and Winnie fit into his plan?

CHAPTER TWENTY

1. Judge the fact that Mae was arrested in light of the fact that the man had been threatening Winnie.

2. Explain the following simile: Tuck was "like a starving man looking through a window at a banquet."

3. What would be Mae's punishment if the man died?

Vocabulary
Chapters Twenty-One, Twenty-Two, and Twenty-Three

Match the vocabulary words on the left to the definitions on the right. Place the correct letter on each line.

____ 1. murmur   A. conquered; beaten
____ 2. mingled   B. an indistinct sound
____ 3. reliably   C. moisture that diminishes visibility
____ 4. acrid   D. regret
____ 5. exertion   E. sounded
____ 6. defeated   F. mixed together in combination
____ 7. remorse   G. balanced; suspended
____ 8. gentility   H. bitter
____ 9. haze   I. unwillingly
____ 10. reluctantly   J. strenuous effort
____ 11. chimed   K. dependably
____ 12. poised   L. refinement

Create a Dialog

In Chapter 22, Jesse gives Winnie a bottle of water from the spring. Suppose Mae, Tuck, or Miles finds out. Create a dialogue between Jessie and one or more members of his family. Use some vocabulary words from the first part of this activity.

© 1996 Educational Impressions, Inc.

Comprehension and Discussion Questions
Chapters Twenty-One, Twenty-Two, and Twenty-Three

Answer the following questions in complete sentence form. Give examples from the story to support your response.

CHAPTER TWENTY-ONE

1. Why did Winnie's family feel as though "some part of her had slipped away"? How had Winnie changed?

2. Why was the news about the man dying both good and bad?

3. To what did Winnie compare Mae's killing of the man? Compare and contrast the two events.

CHAPTER TWENTY-TWO

1. Describe Miles's plan. What was the drawback of the plan?

2. What did Jesse give to Winnie?

3. How did Winnie offer to help rescue Mae?

CHAPTER TWENTY-THREE

1. How did Winnie rationalize her involvement in the escape plan? Have you ever used this excuse to do something you knew you shouldn't do?

2. How did Winnie get her mind off the horror of Mae's predicament?

3. Predict whether or not Winnie will drink the water when she turns seventeen. Explain.

Vocabulary
Chapters Twenty-Four, Twenty-Five, and Epilogue

Choose the word in each set that is **most like** the first word in meaning.

1. **verandah:**   porch   swing   window
2. **accuse:**   excuse   blame   reveal
3. **advantage:**   benefit   expertise   luck
4. **furrowed:**   soft   fractured   wrinkled
5. **flailing:**   swinging   flaming   blowing
6. **precisely:**   prematurely   exactly   quickly
7. **wistful:**   melancholy   thoughtless   fearful
8. **profoundly:**   deeply   surely   lavishly

Choose the word in each set that is **most unlike** the first word in meaning.

1. **receded:**   retreated   advanced   diminished
2. **sedately:**   calmly   excitably   firmly
3. **perversely:**   profusely   improperly   correctly
4. **constricted:** compressed   expanded   built
5. **accomplice:**   supervisor   associate   foe
6. **staunchly:**   weakly   faithfully   slyly
7. **revulsion:**   attraction   revolution   disgust
8. **rigid:**   stiff   flexible   hot

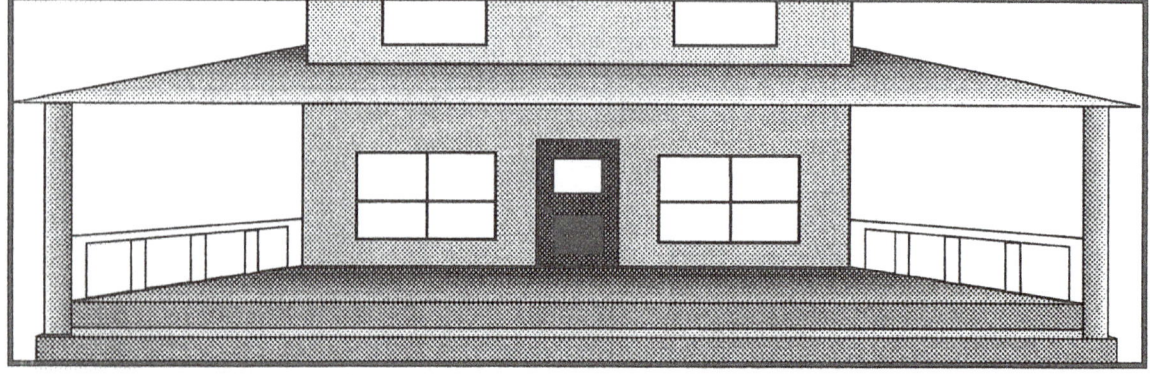

30 *Tuck Everlasting*   © 1996 Educational Impressions, Inc.

Comprehension and Discussion Questions
Chapters Twenty-Four, Twenty-Five, and Epilogue

Answer the following questions in complete sentence form. Give examples from the story to support your response.

CHAPTER TWENTY-FOUR

1. In what way did the weather affect their escape plan?

2. What did Jesse mean when he said, "Remember"?

3. How would you have felt if you had been in Winnie's place at the end of this chapter? Would you have volunteered as she had?

CHAPTER TWENTY-FIVE

1. In your opinion, was Winnie a criminal? Explain.

2. What caused Winnie's family to rally around her?

© 1996 Educational Impressions, Inc.

3. Judge the fact that Winnie poured the water on the toad.

EPILOGUE

1. Mae and Tuck were accustomed to change; nevertheless, these latest changes upset them. Why?

2. What did Tuck learn in the cemetery?

3. What was ironic about Tuck's statement regarding the toad: " 'Durn fool thing must think it's going to live forever' "?

Spotlight Literary Skill
Plot

A **plot** is a sequence of events that tells a story. You have just read *Tuck Everlasting*. Put the following story events in the order as they occurred in the plot. Number the events from 1 to 14. Then rewrite the sentences in their proper order.

____ Tuck visits Winnie's grave.

____ A stranger appears at the Fosters' gate and says he is looking for a family.

____ The stranger offers to tell where Winnie is in exchange for the Fosters' land.

____ Winnie sees Jesse Tuck lift the pebbles and drink from the spring.

____ Mae hits the man in the yellow suit with a shotgun.

____ Mae takes her music box and sets out for Treegap.

____ The constable takes Mae to prison.

____ Jesse gives Winnie a bottle of water from the spring.

____ Winnie talks to the toad about her troubles.

____ Mae, Jesse, and Miles kidnap Winnie.

____ Winnie helps the Tucks free Mae.

____ Winnie's grandmother thinks she hears elf music.

____ Tuck takes Winnie out on the porch and tells her their story.

____ Winnie pours the spring water on the toad.

© 1996 Educational Impressions, Inc.   *Tuck Everlasting* 33

Spotlight Literary Skill
Cause and Effect

Sometimes a certain event or action brings about another event or action. This is what is meant by **cause and effect.** Read the following statement: "But it was the thought of seeing Jesse again that kept Winnie's stomach fluttering." The thought of seeing Jesse is the cause. The fact that Winnie's stomach was fluttering is the effect. In other words, it is thinking about Jessie that causes her stomach to flutter.

Match the causes in the column on the left with the effects in the column on the right. Place the correct letter on each line.

CAUSES

B 1. The Tucks drank from the spring.

D 2. She wanted to be alone.

A 3. Winnie's grandmother said that she had heard the music before.

G 4. Winnie was afraid to go away alone.

H 5. Winnie wanted to find the source of the music.

C 6. They wanted to hide the spring.

E 7. Winnie saw Jesse drink from the spring.

F 8. The stranger threatened to sell the water.

EFFECTS

A. An expression of intense satisfaction came over the stranger's face.

B. The Tucks never aged.

C. The Tucks covered the spring with pebbles.

D. Winnie thought about running away.

E. The Tucks kidnapped Winnie.

F. Mae hit the stranger with a shotgun.

G. Winnie did not run away.

H. Winnie ventured into the wood.

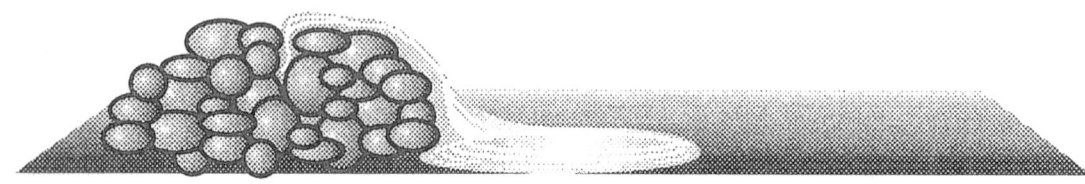

34 *Tuck Everlasting* © 1996 Educational Impressions, Inc.

Spotlight Literary Skill
Similes

A **simile** is a figure of speech that compares two unlike things. The words *like* or *as* are used to make the comparison. Read the following similes which have been taken from the story. Then put them into your own words. For each tell who or what is being described and explain briefly what is happening.

1. "The first week in Autumn hangs...like the highest seat of a Ferris wheel....." (Prologue)

2. "...her backbone felt like a pipe full of cold running water...." (Chapter 6)

3. "It was like a ribbon tying her to familiar things." (Chapter 6)

4. "...Winnie...saw an expression...that made her feel like an unexpected present...." (Chapter 9)

5. "...three armchairs and an elderly rocker stood about aimlessly, like strangers at a party, ignoring each other." (Chapter 10)

6. "...he looked more than ever like a marionette." (Chapter 21)

© 1996 Educational Impressions, Inc.   *Tuck Everlasting* 35

Spotlight Literary Skill
Metaphors

A **metaphor** is a figure of speech that compares two unlike things without the use of the words *like* or *as*. Read the following metaphors which have been taken from the story. Then put them into your own words. For each tell who or what is being described and explain briefly what is happening.

1. "Mae sat there frowning, a great potato of a woman...." (Chapter 2)

_____

_____

_____

2. "...it was as if they had slipped in under a giant colander." (Chapter 9)

_____

_____

_____

3. "The sun was dropping fast now, a soft red sliding egg yolk...." (Chapter 12)

_____

_____

_____

4. "It's a wheel, Winnie." (Chapter 12)

_____

_____

_____

5. "But dying's part of the wheel...." (Chapter 12)

_____

_____

_____

6. "The big glass windows here were lidded eyes...." (Chapter 24)

_____

_____

_____

36 *Tuck Everlasting* © 1996 Educational Impressions, Inc.

Spotlight Literary Skill
Personification

Personification is the bestowing of human qualities on inanimate objects or abstract ideas. Many examples of personification can be found in *Tuck Everlasting*. For example, Natalie Babbitt personified the road in Chapter 1: "It had reason to think where it was going...."

Find at least eight examples of personification in *Tuck Everlasting*. For each, identify the chapter in which you found it.

1. _____

2. _____

3. _____

4. _____

5. _____

6. _____

7. _____

8. _____

Creative-Thinking Activity
What If?

What if Winnie had not poured the water on the toad? What if she had drunk the water when she was seventeen as Jesse had asked her to do? Write a new ending for the story.

Cooperative-Learning Activity
Forever...

With your cooperative-learning group, discuss the pros and cons of remaining forever at various ages. Then have each member of the group decide at which age he or she would remain if given a choice.

AGE	BENEFITS	DISADVANTAGES
10	- young - can do many things - wild - playful	- never get ~~~~ to be an adult - not always helpful
17	- young - playful - more helpful	- not quite old enough to get married - never get to be an adult
25	- an adult - can have a job	- never get to be old
39	- an adult - can have a job ~~~~~~~~~~~~~~	- aren't very playful or wild
49	- an adult - can have a job	- can't do too many things
Other: 4	- ~~~~~ young - wild - playful	- too young to do many things - never get to go to school or become an adult

Share your conclusions with the other groups.

> I think 25 is the best because you can drive, have a job, and your old enough to get married.

© 1996 Educational Impressions, Inc.   *Tuck Everlasting* 39

Post-Reading Activity
To Drink or Not to Drink

Winnie must have done a lot of thinking about whether or not to drink the water. A **soliloquy** is a literary form of expression in which the character reveals his thoughts and feelings when alone or unaware that anyone else is listening. As Winnie, compose a soliloquy in which you describe your feelings and thoughts on your seventeenth birthday. What factors have led to your decision? Are you confident that you are making the right choice?

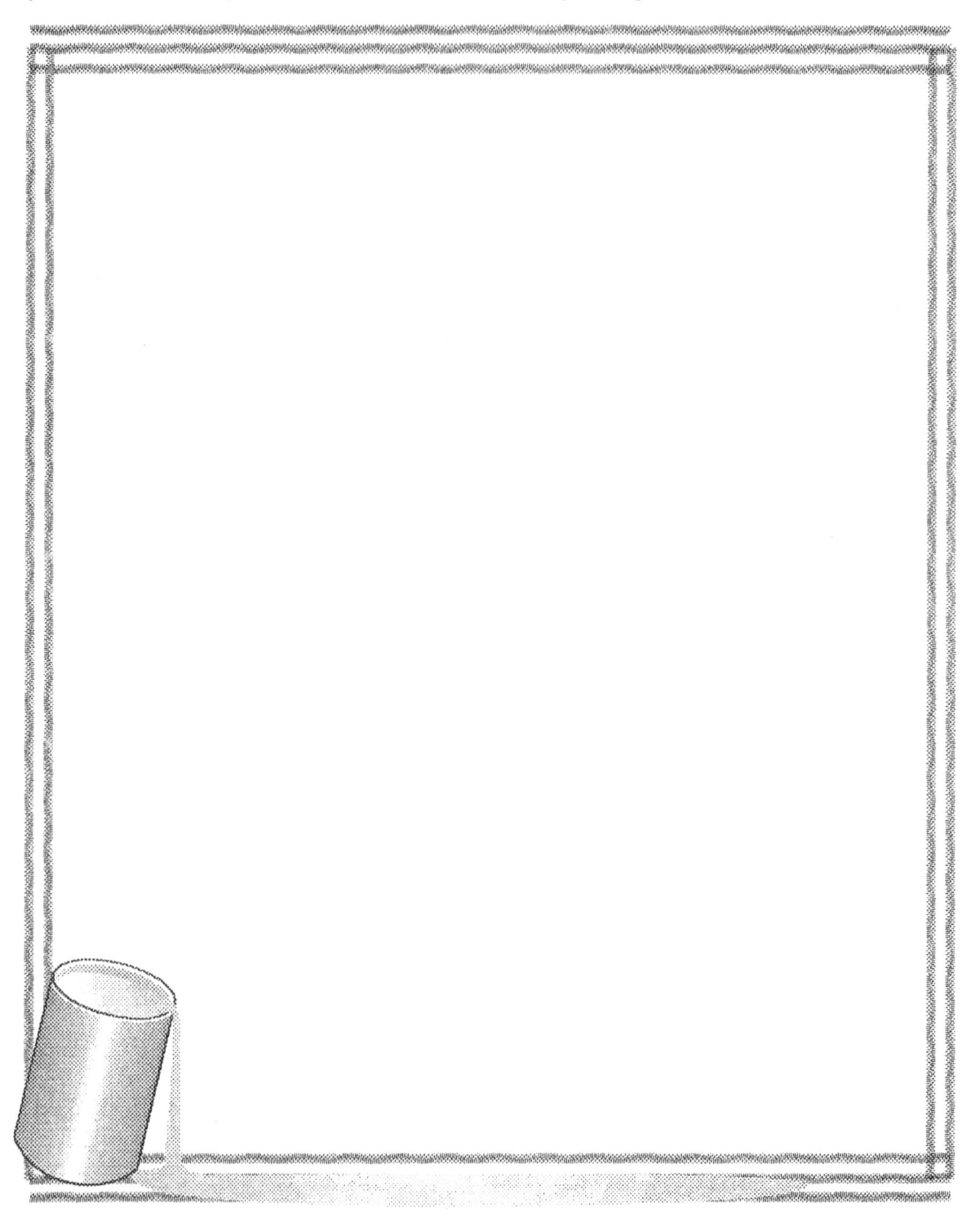

More Post-Reading Activities

1. Using the age you chose in the activity entitled "Forever," brainstorm all the things you would do if you could live forever at that age.

2. Write a letter to the Tucks asking them to share some of their water with you. Cite reasons to convince them that you deserve to live forever.

3. Choose a point of view and write a paragraph explaining why you think eternal life would be a blessing or a curse.

4. Draw pictures of the Tuck family. Use information you read in the novel.

5. Suppose the man in the yellow suit had not been killed. Create a brochure for him to use to market the water. What segment of the population might be a good target audience for his product? Give reasons for your opinion.

6. Create a cartoon from the point of view of the toad one hundred years after Winnie poured the water on it.

7. Create an opening argument to use in defense of Mae Tuck at her murder trial.

© 1996 Educational Impressions, Inc.

Crossword Puzzle
Tuck Everlasting

See how much you remember about *Tuck Everlasting*. Have fun!

Across

3. Jesse's brother.
5. "The house was so proud" is this.
8. Short, concluding section of a book.
9. This family owned the wood at Treegap.
11. "The sun was…a soft…egg yolk" is this.
12. This family was immortal.
13. He remained seventeen.
17. Type of fiction; *Tuck Everlasting* is an example.
18. She was kidnapped by the Tucks.
20. The man in the yellow suit wanted to _____ the water.
22. Animal made immortal by Winnie.
23. Month in which the story begins.

Down

1. To take someone unwilling to go.
2. The source of the Tucks' immortality.
4. Singular form of 19 down.
5. Short introductory section of a book.
6. He arrested Mae.
7. Name of village where story is set.
10. Author of *Tuck Everlasting*.
11. She killed the man in the yellow suit.
12. The Tucks met every _____ years.
14. "Winnie felt like an unexpected present" is this.
15. What Mae carried with her.
16. First name of 10 down.
19. Winnie's grandmother thought they made the music.
21. The Tucks will always remain the same _____.

42   *Tuck Everlasting*   © 1996 Educational Impressions, Inc.

Glossary of Literary Terms

Alliteration: A repetition of initial, or beginning, sounds in two or more consecutive or neighboring words.

Analogy: A comparison based upon the resemblance in some particular ways between things that are otherwise unlike.

Anecdote: A short account of an interesting, amusing or biographical occurrence.

Anticlimax: An event that is less important than what occurred before it.

Archaic language: Language that was once common in a particular historic period but which is no longer commonly used.

Cause and effect: The relationship in which one condition brings about another condition as a direct result. The result, or consequence, is called the effect.

Character development: The ways in which the author shows how a character changes as the story proceeds.

Characterization: The method used by the author to give readers information about a character; a description or representation of a person's qualities or peculiarities.

Classify: To arrange according to a category or trait.

Climax: The moment when the action in a story reaches its greatest conflict.

Compare and contrast: To examine the likenesses and differences of two people, ideas or things. (*Contrast* always emphasizes differences. *Compare* may focus on likenesses alone or on likenesses and differences.)

Conflict: The main source of drama and tension in a literary work; the discord between persons or forces that brings about dramatic action.

Connotation: Something suggested or implied, not actually stated.

Description: An account that gives the reader a mental image or picture of something.

Dialect: A form of language used in a certain geographic region; it is distinguished from the standard form of the language by pronunciation, grammar and/or vocabulary.

Dialogue (dialog): The parts of a literary work that represent conversation.

Fact: A piece of information that can be proven or verified.

Figurative language: Description of one thing in terms usually used for something else. Simile and metaphor are examples of figurative language.

Flashback: The insertion of an earlier event into the normal chronological sequence of a narrative.

Foreshadowing: The use of clues to give readers a hint of events that will occur later on.

Historical fiction: Fiction represented in a setting true to the history of the time in which the story takes place.

Imagery: Language that appeals to the senses; the use of figures of speech or vivid descriptions to produce mental images.

Irony: The use of words to express the opposite of their literal meaning.

Legend: A story handed down from earlier times; its truth is popularly accepted but cannot be verified.

Limerick: A humorous five-lined poem with a specific form: aabba. Lines 1, 2 and 5 are longer than lines 3 and 4.

Metaphor: A figure of speech that compares two unlike things without the use of like or as.

Mood: The feeling that the author creates for the reader.

Motivation: The reasons for the behavior of a character.

Narrative: The type of writing that tells a story.

Narrator: The character who tells the story.

Opinion: A personal point of view or belief.

Parody: Writing that ridicules or imitates something more serious.

Personification: A figure of speech in which an inanimate object or an abstract idea is given human characteristics.

Play: A literary work that is written in dialogue form and that is usually performed before an audience.

Plot: The arrangement or sequence of events in a story.

Point of view: The perspective from which a story is told.

Protagonist: The main character.

Pun: A play on words that are similar in sound but different in meaning.

Realistic fiction: True-to-life fiction; the people, places and happenings are similar to those in real life.

Resolution: The part of the plot from the climax to the ending where the main dramatic conflict is worked out.

Satire: A literary work that pokes fun at individual or societal weaknesses.

Sequencing: The placement of story elements in the order of their occurrence.

Setting: The time and place in which the story occurs.

Simile: A figure of speech that uses *like* or *as* to compare two unlike things.

Stereotype: A character whose personality traits represent a group rather than an individual.

Suspense: Quality that causes readers to wonder what will happen next.

Symbolism: The use of a thing, character, object or idea to represent something else.

Synonyms: Words that are very similar in meaning.

Tall tale: An exaggerated story detailing unbelievable events.

Theme: The main idea of a literary work; the message the author wants to communicate, sometimes expressed as a generalization about life.

Tone: The quality or feeling conveyed by the work; the author's style or manner of expression.

ANSWERS

Prologue and Chapters One and Two: Vocabulary

1. balmy	4. tangent	7. veered	10. forlorn	13. axis
2. quivers	5. fringe	8. ambled	11. grubs	14. melancholy
3. trod	6. bovine	9. meager	12. immense	15. rueful

Prologue: Comprehension and Discussion Questions (Answers may vary.)

1. The expression "dog days" refers to the period from mid-July to September. It is a hot, sultry period—a period of stagnation. The author compared the first week of August to the highest seat on a ferris wheel because everything comes to a standstill—much the way the ferris wheel pauses before its descent.

2. 1) Mae Tuck set out on the trip to the Treegap wood. 2) Winnie Foster, whose family owned the wood, thought about running away. 3) A stranger appeared at the Fosters' gate. The events were connected by the wood.

3. The wood was the hub of the wheel. The wheel represents the story. In a larger sense, the wheel represents life.

Chapter One: Comprehension and Discussion Questions (Answers may vary.)

1. It "had a sleeping, otherworld appearance." It "made you want to speak in whispers." The cows, upon reaching the "sleeping" wood had thought, "Let it keep its peace; *we* won't disturb it." They trod out the road around the wood.

2. "Nothing ever seems interesting when it belongs to you—only when it doesn't."

3. Personification is the attribution of human qualities to inanimate objects. The following are examples of personification. **THE ROAD**: The road "ambled." "...it had reason to think where it was going." "So the road went humbly by...." **THE GRASS**: "...the grass...somewhat...forlorn." **THE HOUSE**: "The house was so proud of itself...." **THE WOOD**: "But the wood had a sleeping...appearance...."

Chapter Two: Comprehension and Discussion Questions (Answers may vary.)

1. He was having a pleasant dream in which the family had never drunk the magical water and were all in heaven.

2. Mae took her music box because it was the only pretty thing she owned; she always took it with her.

3. We learned that the Tucks had remained the same age for 87 years. Clues include the following: "Nothing's going to change." (Mae) "It's ten years since I went to Treegap." (Mae) We already knew that she made the trip every ten years. "What in the world could possibly happen to you?" (Tuck)

Chapter Three: Comprehension and Discussion Questions (Answers may vary.)

1. Winnie told her troubles to a toad. Answers will vary, but although the toad couldn't respond, neither could it reprimand her for her thoughts.

2. If she had had a sibling, her mother and grandmother could have focussed some of their attention on her sibling instead of always looking at her.

3. Answers will vary.

Chapter Four: Comprehension and Discussion Questions (Answers may vary.)

1. "Winnie...was suddenly reminded of the stiff black ribbons they had hung on the door of the cottage for her grandfather's funeral."

2. It was music from Mae's music box. She had heard it ten years ago, the last time Mae made her trip to Treegap.

3. Answers will vary, but many will guess that he knew about the Tucks. They may also guess that he was aware of Mae's music box.

Chapter Five: Comprehension and Discussion Questions (Answers may vary.)

1. She wanted to discover the source of the music.

2. They were piled there to conceal the spring. We were first told this at the end of Chapter One.

3. Many will guess that the water is what made the Tucks immortal and that the Tucks had wanted to keep their situation a secret. Jesse had feared that someday someone would learn their secret.

Chapters Six, Seven, and Eight: Vocabulary

1. troupe	3. harness	5. populated	7. conclusion	9. whoop
2. burly	4. knobby	6. graze	8. parson	10. crept

The Tucks had a big secret!

Chapter Six: Comprehension and Discussion Questions (Answers may vary.)

1. In Winnie's visions the kidnappers were rough, burly men. These kidnappers were a gentle family. In Winnie's visions she pleaded for mercy. In reality the kidnappers did the pleading.

2. She realized that this was a real kidnapping and that there was a chance that she'd never see her mother again. When Mae promised to return her tomorrow, it seemed like forever. She wanted to go home.

3. Answers will vary, but perhaps they didn't want to deal with an unpleasant situation. As more and more time passed, they may have begun to believe that their luck would hold out forever.

Chapter Seven: Comprehension and Discussion Questions (Answers may vary.)

1. His wife had left him because he never aged. At forty years of age he looked exactly as he had looked when they were first married and he was twenty-two. She thought that he had sold his soul to the Devil in order to retain his youthful appearance.

2. No harm could come to the Tucks nor to their horse. They did not change. All had drunk the water. Their cat, however, did not drink the water and it died. The tree near the spring hadn't changed either.

3. He shot himself through the heart.

© 1996 Educational Impressions, Inc.

Chapter Eight: Comprehension and Discussion Questions (Answers may vary.)
1. Answers will vary.
2. They made her feel wanted and special—like a friend. They also made her feel older, more mature—perhaps because they were so childlike.
3. The man in the yellow suit had heard everything.

Chapters Nine, Ten, and Eleven: Vocabulary

1. A	5. M	9. T	13. H	17. E
2. D	6. P	10. O	14. C	18. L
3. G	7. R	11. B	15. J	19. I
4. K	8. N	12. S	16. F	20. Q

Chapter Nine: Comprehension and Discussion Questions (Answers may vary.)
1. Mae insisted that she wear her straw hat to block the sun. Miles carried her part of the way.
2. In Chapter 2 we were told that "Tuck almost never smiled except in sleep."
3. At first she felt shy, but Tuck seemed so happy to see her that she soon felt "like an unexpected present...."

Chapter Ten: Comprehension and Discussion Questions (Answers may vary.)
1. It was in a state of disarray: It was dusty. Things were scattered all over the floor. Furniture was set about helter-skelter.
2. They had lived there for twenty years. They couldn't stay in any one place much longer than that because someone might notice that they hadn't changed.
3. Jesse was less responsible. Miles was more serious. Jesse thought their immortality was wonderful. In Chapter 8 he said, "Just think of all the things we're going to see." It was Miles who worried about the effect this could have on Winnie: "That kind of talk'll make her want to...drink a gallon of the stuff....There's a whole lot more to it than Jesse Tuck's good times." Jesse was carefree; he sang funny songs, swung from trees, and showed off.

Chapter Eleven: Comprehension and Discussion Questions (Answers may vary.)
1. They ate in the parlor. They did not sit around a table. Jesse even sat on the floor. They did not use napkins. It was all right to lick one's fingers. There was no conversation.
2. The realization that she was eating with strangers and that she had, in fact, been kidnapped caused her elation to collapse.
3. She believed he would tell her family where he saw her.

Chapter Twelve: Comprehension and Discussion Questions (Answers may vary.)
1. A metaphor is the comparison of two unlike things without the use of *like* or *as*. Tuck compared his family to a rowboat stuck in the branches. The water keeps passing it by, but it is still stuck in one place, unable to move on. Like the rowboat, the Tucks were stuck in one place (in time). Everything around them changed and grew, but they stayed the same.
2. Answers will vary.
3. Answers will vary.

Chapter Thirteen: Comprehension and Discussion Questions (Answers may vary.)
1. They were worried about Winnie.

Chapter Fourteen: Comprehension and Discussion Questions (Answers may vary.)
1. The author wanted to give the readers a hint that something bad was about to happen. Tuck said, "I don't like it. I got a bad feeling about the whole thing."
2. She wanted to be in her own nightgown, in her own bed. She felt exhausted, helpless, and angry.
3. Mae and Tuck each came to comfort her. She felt well cared for and guilty that she had thought of them as criminals. She worried about what would happen to them.
4. Answers will vary.

Chapter Fifteen: Comprehension and Discussion Questions (Answers may vary.)
1. He said that he would tell them where Winnie was only if they agreed to let him have the wood!
2. Answers will vary, but the Fosters made the agreement under duress. Many will probably believe that it was unlikely that they would have been forced to keep their end of the bargain.
3. The man knew about the secret spring. Answers will vary, but some might guess that he wanted it for personal gain.

Chapter Sixteen: Comprehension and Discussion Questions (Answers may vary.)
1. He said that he wanted to follow them to see where they were taking her.
2. The man in the yellow suit told him that the Fosters had sold him their wood. The Fosters were the first family in the area and were considered to be "land-proud."
3. Answers will vary, but most will probably not believe him. We know he had ulterior motives.

Chapter Seventeen: Comprehension and Discussion Questions (Answers may vary.)
1. Answers will vary, but by then Miles may have felt that immortality was as much a curse as a blessing.
2. She couldn't stand the thought of anything dying. She had said, " 'It'd be nice if nothing ever had to die.' "
3. Answers will vary.

Chapters Eighteen, Nineteen, and Twenty: Vocabulary

1. quivering	3. passing	5. course	7. irritability	9. spread	11. holding
2. strange	4. stories	6. uneducated	8. shouted	10. bitterly	12. rough

Chapter Eighteen: Comprehension and Discussion Questions (Answers may vary.)
1. She was infatuated with Jesse. She was probably thinking about his suggestion that she drink the water when she turns seventeen.
2. Tuck "was the dearest of them all" to her. Answers will vary, but in Chapter 9, when Winnie first met Tuck, he "made her feel like an unexpected present." In other words, he made her feel special, like something he really wanted but didn't think he would have.
3. It was the first caller they had had in the twenty years they had lived there.

Chapter Nineteen: Comprehension and Discussion Questions (Answers may vary.)
1. His grandmother had told him stories about an odd family whose members never aged. His grandmother had been a friend of Miles's wife.
2. The tune in the music box was the man's means of identifying the mother of the family that didn't grow old. If he hadn't heard the melody, he might not have discovered the Tucks.
3. He planned to drink the water himself and to sell the water to rich people, people whom he considered "deserving" of the water. He planned to use the Tucks to demonstrate the powers of the water. When the Tucks made it clear they wouldn't cooperate, he decided to use Winnie instead. He would force her to drink the water and then use her for his demonstrations.

Chapter Twenty: Comprehension and Discussion Questions (Answers may vary.)
1. Answers will vary.
2. A simile is the comparison of two unlike things using *like* or *as*. The man appeared to be dying, and Tuck was envious.
3. Mae would be hanged; however, she would not die.

Chapters Twenty-One, Twenty-Two, and Twenty-Three: Vocabulary
1. B	3. K	5. J	7. D	9. C	11. E
2. F	4. H	6. A	8. L	10. I	12. G

Chapter Twenty-One: Comprehension and Discussion Questions (Answers may vary.)
1. She was no longer their little girl. Until then, all of her experiences were connected in some way to her family. Although she still had strong feelings for her family, she had also experienced things that had nothing to do with them. She had matured.
2. It was good because the Fosters would still own the wood and because the man would not be able to tell the Tucks' secret. It was bad because Mae would be charged with murder and sentenced to be hanged.
3. She compared it to the time she had killed a wasp. Winnie had killed the wasp out of fear for her own safety. Mae killed the man out of fear for Winnie's safety and for the safety of the world at large. Winnie's act was not a crime; Mae's was. Winnie regretted her act. Mae probably did not, for she did not have much choice.

Chapter Twenty-Two: Comprehension and Discussion Questions (Answers may vary.)
1. When it got dark, he would take the window frame out of the jail wall so that Mae could climb through the opening. The drawback was that the constable would probably notice right away that she was gone and would chase after her.
2. He gave her a bottle of water from the spring. He wanted her to save it until she was seventeen and then drink it and find them.
3. She offered to climb in when Mae climbed out and to wrap herself in Mae's blanket so that the constable wouldn't notice immediately that Mae was missing.

Chapter Twenty-Three: Comprehension and Discussion Questions (Answers may vary.)
1. She could say, "Well, you never told me *not* to go!"
2. She thought about Jesse and the water he had given her.
3. Answers will vary.

Chapters Twenty-Four, Twenty-Five, and Epilogue: Vocabulary
PART 1
1. porch	3. benefit	5. swinging	7. melancholy
2. blame	4. wrinkled	6. exactly	8. deeply

PART 2
1. advanced	3. correctly	5. foe	7. attraction
2. excitably	4. expanded	6. weakly	8. flexible

Chapter Twenty-Four: Comprehension and Discussion Questions (Answers may vary.)
1. It helped. The sound of thunder muffled the sound of Miles working on the window. It also muffled the sound of Jesse's laughter.
2. He wanted Winnie to think about the bottle of water he had given her.
3. Answers will vary.

Chapter Twenty-Five: Comprehension and Discussion Questions (Answers may vary.)
1. Answers will vary.
2. Winnie told them that she had helped the Tucks because she loved them.
3. Answers will vary.

Epilogue: Comprehension and Discussion Questions (Answers may vary.)
1. They were used to gradual change, but these changes were drastic.
2. He learned that Winnie had married and that she had had at least one child. He learned that she had died in 1948 at the age of 78.
3. It *was* going to live forever! Winnie had poured the spring water on it.

Spotlight Literary SKill: Plot
14, 3, 8, 5, 9, 1, 10, 11, 2, 6, 12, 4, 7, and 13.

Spotlight Literary Skill: Cause and Effect
1. B   2. D   3. A   4. G   5. H   6. C   7. E   8. F

Spotlight Literary Skill: Similes
1. The first week in autumn is compared to the top seat on a Ferris wheel because everything seems to pause—like the wheel pauses before its descent.
2. Winnie's backbone is compared to a cold pipe because she got a chill down her spine.
3. The music from Mae's music box is compared to a ribbon tying Winnie to familiar things because Winnie and her grandmother had heard and discussed the music earlier.
4. Winnie is compared to an unexpected present because Tuck seemed so happy and surprised to see her.
5. The furniture is compared to strangers because the pieces didn't seem to have anything to do with each other the way they were scattered about.
6. The man in the yellow suit is compared to a marionette because his arms and legs were sprawled every which way.

Spotlight Literary Skill: Metaphors
1. Mae is compared to a potato because of her physical appearance.
2. The trees are compared to a colander because of the way they drooped.
3. The sun is compared to an egg yolk because of the way it looked when it was setting.
4. The water cycle is compared to a wheel. "Everything's a wheel, turning and turning, never stopping."
5. The life cycle is compared to a wheel that keeps turning.
6. The windows are compared to eyes that are closed. It was dark and it didn't seem like anyone in the houses was interested in what they were doing.

Spotlight Literary Skill: Personification
Some examples are as follows:
CHAPTER 1
The grass [was] forlorn.
A capable iron fence...said, "Move on—we don't want *you* here."
The road went humbly by....
The house was so proud....
CHAPTER 2
She pulled down...a blue straw hat with a drooping, exhausted brim.
CHAPTER 5
The sun was only just opening its own eye....
CHAPTER 6
Disconnected thoughts presented themselves...as if they had been waiting their turn....
CHAPTER 9
The graceful arms of the pines stretched out....
CHAPTER 10
Three armchairs and an elderly rocker stood about aimlessly....
CHAPTER 11
The pond's got answers.
CHAPTER 17
The first week of August was reasserting itself....
CHAPTER 23
The countryside, the village of Treegap, the wood—all lay defeated.
The sun sank reluctantly....
The night seemed poised on tiptoe...holding its breath for the storm.
A fourth nail screeched....

Crossword Puzzle

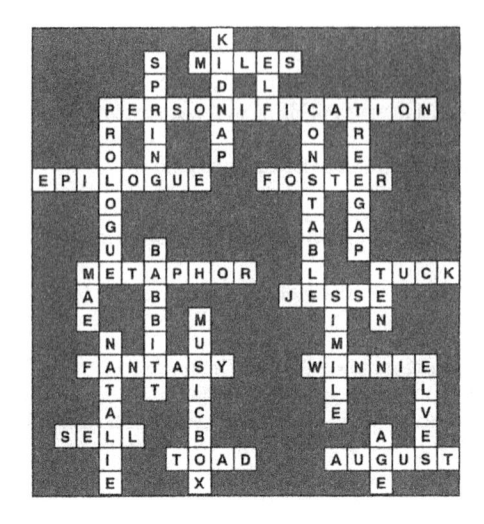